# THE CANTERVILLE GHOST

Most grand old houses have a family ghost of some kind. Sometimes it is a quiet and kindly ghost, and sometimes it is a noisy one, always banging doors and crashing about in chains.

The ghost at Canterville Chase is one of the noisy kind, and the family can't get any sleep at night. So Lord Canterville sells the house to Mr Hiram B. Otis, who is an American and not at all worried about ghosts. In fact, Mr and Mrs Otis and their children – Washington, pretty Virginia, and the twins, two noisy little boys – are very happy to live in a house with a ghost.

But the ghost is not happy. His job is to frighten people, and the Otis family aren't frightened by any of his best tricks. Their hair doesn't turn white, they don't run away in terror, they don't faint – they don't even scream! And the Otis twins know more tricks than the poor ghost will ever know . . .

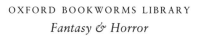

OXFORD BOOKWORMS LIBRARY
*Fantasy & Horror*

# The Canterville Ghost

Stage 2 (700 headwords)

Series Editor: Jennifer Bassett
Founder Editor: Tricia Hedge
Activities Editors: Jennifer Bassett and Christine Lindop

OSCAR WILDE

# The Canterville Ghost

*Retold by*
John Escott

*Illustrated by*
Summer Durantz

OXFORD UNIVERSITY PRESS

# OXFORD
### UNIVERSITY PRESS

Great Clarendon Street, Oxford OX2 6DP

Oxford University Press is a department of the University of Oxford.
It furthers the University's objective of excellence in research, scholarship,
and education by publishing worldwide in

Oxford New York

Auckland Cape Town Dar es Salaam Hong Kong Karachi
Kuala Lumpur Madrid Melbourne Mexico City Nairobi
New Delhi Shanghai Taipei Toronto

With offices in

Argentina Austria Brazil Chile Czech Republic France Greece
Guatemala Hungary Italy Japan Poland Portugal Singapore
South Korea Switzerland Thailand Turkey Ukraine Vietnam

OXFORD and OXFORD ENGLISH are registered trade marks of
Oxford University Press in the UK and in certain other countries

ISBN 978 0 19 479053 6

A complete recording of this Bookworms edition of
*The Canterville Ghost* is available on audio CD ISBN 978 0 19 478976 9

Printed in China

*Illustrations by*: Summer Durantz of Advocate

Word count (main text): 6100 words

For more information on the Oxford Bookworms Library,
visit www.oup.com/bookworms

# CONTENTS

# 1

## THE OTIS FAMILY COMES TO CANTERVILLE

When Hiram B. Otis, the American businessman, bought the house called Canterville Chase, people told him that he was doing a very dangerous thing. Everybody knew that there was a ghost in the house. Lord Canterville himself told Mr Otis all about it.

'We don't like to live in the house ourselves,' he said. 'Too many of my family have seen the ghost. My wife's grandmother, the Duchess of Bolton, is one of them. One night, while she was dressing for dinner, two skeleton

*'We don't like to live in the house ourselves,' Lord Canterville said.*

1

hands were put on her shoulders. She has been ill for years because of that. And my wife never got any sleep there, because of all the noises at night.'

'Lord Canterville,' answered Mr Otis, 'I will buy both the house *and* the ghost. I come from a modern country, and we can buy nearly everything in America – but not ghosts. So, if there really *is* a ghost in the house, we can send it home to America, and people will pay to go and see it.'

'I'm afraid that the house really *does* have a ghost,' said Lord Canterville, smiling. 'Perhaps there are no ghosts in *your* country, but our ghost has been in the house for three hundred years, and it always appears before the death of one of the family.'

'Well, so does the family doctor, Lord Canterville. But there are no ghosts, sir, in *any* country – not even in famous old British families.'

'Very well,' said Lord Canterville. 'If you're happy to have a ghost in the house, that's all right. But please remember that I *did* tell you about it.'

\* \* \*

And so Mr Hiram B. Otis bought the house, and a few weeks later he and his family went down to Canterville Chase on the train.

Mrs Otis was a very beautiful woman, and looked just as English as an Englishwoman. American people are really no different from English people – but they do, of course, speak a different language. Her eldest son, Washington, was a good-looking young man with a wonderful smile, who was famous at all the London parties for his fine dancing. Miss Virginia E. Otis was a sweet little girl of fifteen with big blue eyes. She loved to ride horses and could ride faster than a lot of men. One day the young Duke of Cheshire saw her on horseback, and immediately asked her to marry him – but his family sent him back to school the next day. After Virginia came the twins – two happy, noisy little boys, who were always laughing and playing tricks.

It was a lovely July evening when the family got off the train. The fields and trees looked beautiful in the golden sunshine. The birds were singing sweetly, and the sky was a bright blue. But when they arrived at Canterville Chase, storm clouds suddenly appeared in the sky. Then ten or twelve large black birds flew down over their heads, and big drops of rain began to fall.

An old woman in a black dress was standing in the doorway of the house, waiting to meet them. This was Mrs Umney, the housekeeper.

'Welcome to Canterville Chase,' she said.

They followed her into the library – a long, dark room with a high window at one end. Here, tea was ready for them, so they took off their coats and sat down.

*Mrs Umney, the housekeeper, was waiting to meet them.*

Suddenly Mrs Otis saw a dark red stain on the floor, near the fireplace.

'Is that a stain on the floor there?' she asked.

'Yes, Mrs Otis,' said Mrs Umney quietly. 'It's a bloodstain.'

'Oh, that's terrible!' cried Mrs Otis. 'I can't have bloodstains on my floors. It must go.'

The old woman smiled, and again answered in a quiet voice. 'It is the blood of Lady Eleanore de Canterville,' she said. 'Her husband, Sir Simon de Canterville, murdered her in 1575, while she was standing just *there*, in that place. He lived for another nine years after her death, but then he disappeared, very strangely and suddenly. Nobody ever found his body, but his ghost is still in the house, and will not rest. The bloodstain is famous – visitors come here specially to see it. People have tried to clean it, but it will not go away.'

'Of course it will!' cried Washington Otis. 'Pinkerton's Famous Stain Cleaner will clean it up in a second.'

And before the housekeeper could stop him, he was cleaning the floor with a small black stick.

A minute later, the bloodstain was gone!

'There you are!' he said, smiling at the others. 'Pinkerton can clean anything!'

But at these words the storm outside suddenly began. A terrible flash of lightning lit up the room, and a second later came a great crash of thunder. Everyone jumped up at the sound of the thunder . . . and Mrs Umney fainted.

'What terrible weather this country has!' said Mr Otis. He sat down again and lit a cigarette.

Mrs Umney lay on the floor, with her eyes closed. Mrs

*'There you are!' said Washington. 'Pinkerton can clean anything.'*

Otis looked at her. 'My dear Hiram,' she cried. 'What can we do with a woman who faints?'

'Tell her she has to pay some money,' said Mr Otis. 'If she breaks a cup or something, she has to pay for it. So tell her to pay if she faints. She won't faint after that.'

At this Mrs Umney immediately sat up, but she looked very unhappy. 'Be careful! Trouble is coming to this house!' she said, her voice shaking. 'I have seen things here which are too terrible to describe. For night after night, I have not closed my eyes in sleep.'

Mr Otis gave her a warm smile. 'My wife and I are not afraid of ghosts, Mrs Umney.'

The old housekeeper got shakily to her feet. 'You Americans are so strong!' she said. 'And so kind! You know, I have worked here for many, many years at the same pay, and . . .'

'OK, Mrs Umney. We'll pay you more money,' said Mr Otis, still smiling.

'Oh, thank you, dear Mr Otis. And dear Mrs Otis. Thank you very much.'

# 2

## SIR SIMON MEETS THE OTIS FAMILY

The storm went on all night, and the next morning, when the family came down to breakfast, the bloodstain was on the library floor again.

'That's strange,' said Washington. 'Pinkerton's Famous Stain Cleaner usually cleans anything. It must be the ghost.'

He cleaned the floor again with the little black stick, but the next morning the stain appeared once more. That night, Mr Otis closed the windows and locked the library door. But in the morning the bloodstain was there again.

The family found this most interesting.

'Is there a ghost, or isn't there?' they said to themselves. They could not decide.

But that night, they had the answer to their question.

After the family was in bed and asleep, a strange noise woke Mr Otis. It sounded like something metal moving slowly along the passage, and it was coming nearer to his bedroom door. He got out of bed and listened carefully. The strange noise went on, and he also heard the sound of footsteps. Then he put on his shoes, took a small bottle from his cupboard, and opened the door of his room.

There, in the moonlight, was an old man with eyes as red as fire. His grey hair was long and dirty, his clothes were old and full of holes, and there were heavy metal chains round his arms and legs.

'My dear man,' said Mr Otis, 'you really must put some oil on those noisy chains! I've brought you a bottle of Tammany's Sun Oil, which is very good. Everybody in America uses it. I'll leave it here for you, and I'll be happy to give you some more when you need it.'

*'You really must put some oil on those noisy chains!' said Mr Otis.*

He put the bottle down on a small table, then went back inside his room and got into bed.

For a second or two the Canterville ghost stood still. He was so angry! Then he knocked the bottle of oil on to the floor and hurried away. A strange green light came from his body, and he gave a long and terrible cry that rang through the house. But when he got to the top of the stairs, a door opened, two little people appeared, and a large pillow went flying past his head!

This was too much for the ghost, so he quickly disappeared through the wall, and soon the house was quiet again.

When he got to his secret room, the Canterville ghost sat down in the moonlight and tried to think. He was both angry and unhappy.

'For three hundred years,' he said to himself, 'I have been the best and the most famous ghost in the country! Everybody – *everybody* – has been afraid of me. There was the Duchess of Bolton not long ago. I put my skeleton hands on her shoulders, and she nearly died of terror. She has been ill ever since. Before that, there were three – no, four – housekeepers, who ran away from the house, screaming. Then there was that wonderful night in 1752 when Lord Augustus shot himself in the library, because he saw a skeleton in the armchair by the fire. And there was the beautiful Lady Stutfield, who never spoke

*Lord Augustus shot himself in the library, because he saw
a skeleton in the armchair.*

again after my cold fingers held her long white neck while
she sat at dinner.'

The ghost sat there, remembering all those happy
times in the past. But he was not happy now. 'After all
this,' he said, 'these terrible modern Americans come to
the house and give me Tammany's Sun Oil for my chains,
and throw pillows at my head! It's too bad! They'll be
sorry for this – oh, yes, they will!'

All night long, the ghost sat, and thought hard.

# 3

## A SECOND GHOST APPEARS AT CANTERVILLE

The next morning, when the Otis family met at breakfast, they talked about the ghost for some time. Mr Otis was a little cross to find the bottle of Tammany's Sun Oil lying on the floor of the passage.

'I don't want,' he said, 'to hurt the ghost in any way.' Here he looked at the boys. 'We must remember that he has lived in this house for a very long time, so I don't think it's very nice to throw pillows at him – no, don't laugh, boys, it's not funny. But if the ghost won't use the oil, we will have to take his chains away from him. We can't possibly sleep with that noise going on outside our bedrooms every night.'

But for the rest of the week all was quiet. The only interesting thing was the bloodstain. Every day Washington cleaned the floor with Pinkerton's Stain Cleaner, and every night Mr Otis carefully locked the windows and the library door. But the bloodstain was always there again the next morning.

It also changed colour a few times. On some days it

was red, on other days it was purple, and once it was bright green. Most of the family thought these colour changes were very funny and they hurried downstairs each morning to find out the new colour. The only person who did not laugh was little Virginia, but she would not explain why. And on the morning the bloodstain was bright green, she nearly cried.

On Sunday night, soon after the family went to bed, the ghost made his next move. There was a three-hundred-year-old suit of armour downstairs. 'Now, a ghost in armour will surely frighten even modern Americans,' he thought. He began to put on the suit of armour, but it was too heavy for him, and he and some of the armour fell to the floor with a loud CRASH.

All the men in the Otis family jumped out of bed and hurried downstairs at once. They found the unhappy ghost sitting there, holding his head and crying softly with pain. The twins had their pea-shooters with them and immediately began to shoot little balls of paper at him. Mr Otis brought out his handgun and, like the good Californian he was, called out to the ghost:

'Hold up your hands!'

At this, the ghost jumped up with a wild and angry scream and flew through them. Washington Otis's candle went out, and suddenly everything was dark. At the top of the stairs, the ghost turned to give his terrible ghostly laugh – the famous laugh which once turned Lord Raker's hair white in a single night. It went on and on until the house was full of the sound.

A bedroom door opened and Mrs Otis appeared with a bottle in her hand. 'I'm afraid you're not feeling very

*Mr Otis called out to the ghost: 'Hold up your hands!'*

well,' she said to the ghost. 'I've brought you some of Dr Dobell's special stomach medicine. If you're having trouble with your stomach, this will soon help you to feel better.'

The ghost looked at her angrily, and began to turn himself into a big black dog (one of his most famous tricks). But the sound of young footsteps coming up the stairs stopped him, and he quickly disappeared with a ghostly 'Oooooooh!' before the twins arrived at the top.

For some days after this he was very ill, and only went out to make the bloodstain again each night. But when he began to feel better, he decided to try for the third time to frighten Hiram B. Otis and his family.

He spent most of Friday, the 17th of August, trying to decide what to wear. At last he decided on a dead man's shroud, a large black hat with a red feather in it, and a long knife.

That night the wind shook all the doors and windows, and the rain crashed down on to the roof of the house. The ghost made his plans carefully.

'I'll go first to Washington Otis's room,' he said to himself. 'He cleans away the famous Canterville bloodstain each morning, so I want to be sure that he'll be really frightened. I'll make ghostly noises to wake him up, then I'll push my knife into my neck three times, to the sound of slow music.

'Then I'll go to Mr Hiram B. Otis's room. I'll make a terrible noise in his ear, and at the same time put my cold hand on Mrs Otis's face. Now, what about Virginia? She's never played any tricks on me, and she's sweet and pretty. Perhaps I'll just make a soft 'Ooooh!' in her ear . . . or move her bed sheets a little with my skeleton's fingers.

'And then on to the twins! Those horrible boys are going to learn a lesson tonight! I'll stand between their beds, looking like a dead body – cold and green and

*'I'll push my knife into my neck three times,'*
*said the ghost to himself.*

16

smelling of death. They'll be too frightened to move. Then I'll throw off my shroud and do my famous skeleton dance all round the room.'

He heard the family go to bed at half-past ten. For some time he listened to the laughs and shouts of the twins, but by a quarter past eleven all was quiet.

At the sound of midnight, the ghost left his room. He came out of the wall with the knife in his hand and a smile on his face. It was not a nice smile, and when the moon saw it through a window, she hid behind a cloud.

Slowly and silently the ghost moved through the house, while the Otis family went on happily sleeping. At the corner of the passage which went along to Washington's room, the ghost stopped for a minute. A little wind came from nowhere, pulling his long white shroud this way and that, and showing the skeleton arms and neck of the walking dead. He heard the clock sound a quarter past midnight, gave a little laugh, and turned the corner . . .

. . . And stopped – in terror! There, in front of him, was standing the most horrible ghost. It had a large head with no hair on it, and a fat round face with a deathly smile across its open mouth. A red light burned like fire inside its mouth and behind both of its eyes. Its great body was hidden under a long shroud, and it carried a large piece of paper with strange writing on it.

*There, in front of him, was standing the most horrible ghost.*

The Canterville ghost did not wait to read it. He was too frightened. When you see your first ghost, you don't stop to talk, you turn and run – so the Canterville ghost turned and ran. His long shroud got caught around his feet and he nearly fell over, but he ran as fast as he could, away from the horrible thing that was watching him with fire in its eyes. He turned the corner, dropped his knife into one of Hiram B. Otis's shoes, which were outside his bedroom door (Mr Otis found it there the next morning), and ran on to his room.

He threw himself onto his bed, and hid his head under his pillow. It was some time before he began to feel better. Then he told himself that he was a Canterville, and that Cantervilles were fighters to the end.

'When it gets light,' he thought, 'I'll go and speak to this other ghost. Perhaps we can be friends. After all, two ghosts are better than one, and if the two of us work together, perhaps we can frighten those terrible twins at last.'

Very early the next morning, while the family was still sleeping, he went back to the passage. The other ghost was still there, but now there was something wrong with it. There was no fire in its eyes, and it was resting against the wall like a sick man. The Canterville ghost moved forward quickly and put his arms round the other ghost – and its head fell off! Then the body fell to the floor, and the Canterville ghost saw that he was holding a white bed sheet. And there was a brush, and a turnip with holes in it, lying at his feet.

'What's happened?' he thought. 'Where has the ghost gone?'

Then he saw the piece of paper on the front of the sheet, and there, in the grey morning light, he read these terrible words:

The Otis Ghost
The only true and real ghost
All others are false.

At once he understood everything. It was a trick – another horrible trick! He stood there, too angry to move, and tried to think of a plan to finish these terrible Americans once and for all. But he couldn't think of any plan, so after a while he went to find a quiet dark place to lie down in.

# 4

## ENEMIES EVERYWHERE!

For the next five days the ghost stayed in his room. He was very tired, and he didn't feel well. He decided to stop putting the bloodstain on the library floor.

'The Otis family don't want it,' he thought, 'so they're not going to have it!'

Ghostly appearances were different, of course. It was his job to appear in the passage once a week, and to 'Oooooh!' and 'Aaaaagh!' from the great window on the stairs on the first and third Wednesday in every month.

So for the next three Saturdays, as usual, he walked along the passages between midnight and three o'clock. But he didn't want anybody to see or hear him. He took off his shoes and walked as quietly as he could. He wore a large black coat, and was careful to use Tammany's Sun Oil on his chains. At first he didn't want to, but one evening, while the family was at dinner, he went into Mr Otis's bedroom and took the bottle. After a time, he saw that the oil was really very useful.

But the twins still went on with their tricks. They put

*One night he went crashing down the stairs to the bottom.*

things in his way in dark corners, and he fell over them. They put butter on the top stair, and one night his feet went from under him and he went crashing down the stairs to the bottom. This made him very angry, and he decided to visit the boys the next night, as the famous 'Duke With No Head', and frighten them half to death.

He spent three hours getting ready, and was very pleased with how he looked. At a quarter past one he walked through the wall and moved silently through the passages to the twins' bedroom.

The door was open a little way. Pushing it hard, the ghost walked into the room – and a heavy jug of water fell right down on him. At the same time, he heard the twins laughing in their beds.

The ghost – wet from top to bottom – turned and ran from the room. He did not stop until he was back in his room. The next day he was ill with a bad cold.

After this, the ghost stopped trying to frighten the American family. He walked silently round the passages in soft shoes, carrying an old gun, and tried to stay away from everyone.

The last of the tricks happened on the 19th of September. That night the ghost was wearing one of his favourite shrouds, and he decided to walk down to the library. He wanted to see what was left of the bloodstain. He was on his way there when two shapes jumped out of a dark corner of the passage and shouted 'BOO!' in his ear.

The ghost was very frightened, of course, and ran to the stairs. But Washington Otis was waiting for him there, with a big garden-syringe. There were enemies on all sides! 'Aaaagh!' the ghost cried, then turned quickly and disappeared into the fireplace, which, luckily for him, was not lit. When at last he got back to his room, he was terribly dirty, with black all over his favourite shroud, and very unhappy.

After this, nobody saw him again at night. The twins waited to play tricks on him three or four times. They put nutshells all along the passages, which made walking around difficult for everyone in the house, but the ghost did not appear.

'Oh dear, he's too unhappy to come out,' they said.

Mr Otis began work again on his book. Mrs Otis gave a number of big 'American parties' for the English people who lived near them. The boys played in the house and garden, and Virginia went horse-riding with the young Duke of Cheshire. He was staying at Canterville Chase for the last week of his holidays.

Mr Otis wrote a letter to Lord Canterville and said: 'We think that the ghost has gone away.'

And Lord Canterville wrote back: 'I am happy to hear it!'

*There were enemies on all sides!*

But Mr Otis was wrong. The ghost was still in the house. It is true that he was ill, but he was not yet ready to stop his ghostly work. The young Duke of Cheshire was staying in the house, and the ghost knew the Duke's family well. He once appeared before the brother of the Duke's grandfather as the Horseman of Death. The poor man's hair turned white in one night, and for the rest of his life he could only say the words, 'Turn out the light, turn out the light.' Now the ghost wanted to do the Horseman of Death for the young Duke too.

He got everything ready, but in the end he never left his room. He was too frightened of the twins to go out, and the young Duke slept happily in his bed, thinking of pretty Virginia.

# 5

## POOR, POOR GHOST!

A few days after this, Virginia and the young Duke went out horse-riding. They were riding through some woods when one of the trees caught Virginia's skirt and made a big hole in it. Later, when she got home, she went up the back stairs to her room. She wanted to change her skirt before anyone saw it.

On the way to her bedroom she went past a room which was not often used. The door was half open, and she stopped. 'Is someone in there?' she thought. She went to the door and looked in.

To her surprise, Virginia saw the Canterville ghost. He was sitting near the window, watching the first leaves of autumn dancing in the wind. His head was on his hand, and he looked very unhappy. At first, little Virginia wanted to run away and lock herself in her room, but then she began to feel sorry for him.

She went quietly into the room, but he did not see her until she spoke. 'I am so sorry for you,' she said. 'But my brothers are going back to school tomorrow, and then

*'Stop!' cried Virginia. 'It is you who are horrible.'*

nobody will hurt you if you don't try to frighten us.'

The ghost was also surprised to see Virginia. 'But I am a ghost,' he answered. 'I *must* walk about at night, shake my chains, and go "Oooooh!" and "Aaaaagh!" through keyholes. That's my job. It's why I'm here.'

'It's not why at all,' said Virginia. 'And you have been very bad. Mrs Umney told us that you killed your wife.'

'Well, that's true,' said the ghost.

'It is very wrong to kill anyone,' Virginia told him.

'Oh, that's very easy to say!' said the ghost. 'My wife was not beautiful like you. And she was a bad housekeeper, and knew nothing about cooking. Well, it doesn't matter now. It's all finished. But I don't think it was very nice of her brothers to kill me.'

'They killed you?' said Virginia.

'Well, they locked me in a room without food or water until I died,' said the ghost.

'No food? Oh, Mr Ghost, I mean, Sir Simon, are you hungry? I have a sandwich – would you like it?'

'No, thank you,' said the Canterville ghost. 'I never eat anything now. But it's very kind of you. You are much nicer than the rest of your horrible family.'

'Stop!' cried Virginia, angrily. 'It is you who are horrible. You took the paints out of my paint box to make that stupid bloodstain in the library. You took my best reds, so I can't make any more pictures of the sun

29

going down in the evenings. Then you took the green and the yellow. What's left? Dark blue and white! What pictures can I make with those? Only moonlight pictures, which are not easy to do. I never said a word about it to the others, but I was very angry. And it was all very stupid. Green blood! *I've* never seen green blood.'

'Well, what could I do?' said the ghost. 'It's very difficult to get real blood these days. And your brother started it all with his Pinkerton's Famous Stain Cleaner, so I used your paint. What's wrong with that? You Americans don't understand anything.'

'You know nothing about Americans or America,' said Virginia. 'Why don't you go there? Father will be very happy to pay for your ticket. There are people in America who are ready to pay a hundred thousand dollars to get a family ghost.'

'No, thank you,' said the ghost. 'I don't think I would like America.'

'Why? Because it doesn't have any old buildings that are falling down? Because everything is new and modern? Or because the people don't speak nicely?' Virginia was angry. 'Excuse me, but I must go and ask my father to give the twins another week's holiday!'

'Please don't go, Miss Virginia,' cried the ghost. 'I am so lonely and so unhappy, and I don't know what to do. I want to go to sleep, but I cannot.'

'That's stupid! You just go to bed and put out your candle. It's very easy to sleep. Even babies can do it, and they're not very clever.'

'I have not slept for three hundred years,' he said unhappily, and Virginia's beautiful blue eyes got bigger and bigger with surprise. 'Three hundred years!' he said again. 'And I'm so tired.'

She began to feel sorry for him once more. Her little mouth trembled like the leaves of a flower, and she looked at him kindly. 'Poor, poor ghost,' she said quietly, and moved nearer to him. 'Isn't there anywhere that you can sleep?'

'On the other side of the woods there is a garden,' he answered, with a far-away look in his eyes. 'The grass is long and deep, there are beautiful white flowers, and a bird sings sweetly all night long. The moon looks down, and the big old tree puts out its arms over the sleepers.'

'You – you mean the Garden of Death,' Virginia said softly.

'Yes, Death. Death could be so beautiful. To lie quietly under the ground, with the grass above moving slowly in the wind, and everything silent . . . To have no yesterday, and no tomorrow. To forget time, to have peace, and to be still for ever.' He looked at her. 'You can open the door to Death for me, for Love is always with you, and Love is stronger than Death is.'

31

*'On the other side of the woods there is a garden.'*

Virginia suddenly felt cold, and she began to tremble.

Then the ghost spoke again, and his voice was like a soft wind through the trees. 'Have you ever read the old words on the library window?' he asked.

'Oh, yes, often,' cried the little girl. 'I know them well.

They are painted in strange black letters, and are difficult to read. There are only four lines:

*When a golden girl has prayed for you,*
*And a little child has cried for you,*
*The house will then be quiet and still,*
*And peace will come to Canterville.*

But I don't know what they mean.'

'They mean this,' said the ghost. 'You can pray for me, because I am bad and cannot pray. You can cry for me, and for all the bad things I have done, because I cannot cry. And if you have been sweet and good and kind, Death will be kind to me. Horrible shapes will come to frighten you in the darkness, and you'll hear terrible voices in your ear, but they cannot hurt you. They cannot win the fight against the goodness of a little child.'

Virginia did not answer, and the ghost watched her unhappily. Suddenly she stood up. Her face was very white, and there was a strange light in her eyes. 'I'm not afraid,' she said. 'I'll pray for you to die, and for you to have peace.'

With a small but happy cry, the ghost stood up, took her hand, and kissed it. His fingers were as cold as snow, and his lips burned like fire. Virginia went with him across the dark room. Suddenly the wall opened and

33

there was a great black hole in front of her. A cold wind came out of the darkness, and she could feel something pulling at her dress.

'Come quickly, quickly!' cried the ghost. 'Or it will be too late.'

And in a second the wall closed behind them, and the room was empty.

*'Come quickly, quickly!' cried the ghost.*

# 6

## A SKELETON FINDS REST AT LAST

Ten minutes later, it was time for tea, but Virginia did not come down for it. At first, Mrs Otis did not worry. She knew that Virginia liked to go out into the garden every evening to get flowers for the dinner-table. But at six o'clock she sent the boys out to look for their sister, while she and Mr Otis looked in every room of the house.

At half-past six the boys came back. They could not find Virginia. Then Mr Otis, Washington, and the Duke of Cheshire got their horses and rode out into the woods and fields around Canterville Chase. They looked everywhere, and asked everybody, 'Have you seen Virginia?' But nobody could help them.

Just before midnight, they went back to the house. They were very worried, but Mr Otis told everybody to get some sleep. 'We'll begin again in the morning,' he said, 'and I'll send for some detectives from London.'

They were all standing at the bottom of the stairs when the clock sounded midnight. Suddenly there was a crash, followed by a loud and terrible cry. Thunder shook the house, and the sound of ghostly music came to their ears.

*A secret door opened – and out walked Virginia!*

Then a secret door opened in the wall at the top of the stairs – and out walked Virginia! She was very white, and she had a little box in her hands.

Everyone ran up the stairs. Mrs Otis threw her arms round her, the Duke of Cheshire kissed her again and again, and the twins laughed and danced around her.

'Where have you been?' said Mr Otis. 'We've looked everywhere for you, and your mother has been so frightened for you. You must never play these tricks again.'

36

'Only on the ghost!' shouted the twins, laughing.

'You must never leave my side again, my dearest Virginia,' said Mrs Otis, and she kissed the trembling child.

'Father,' said Virginia, 'I have been with the ghost. He is dead, and you must come and see him. He was a bad man, but he was really sorry for everything that he did. And look, he gave me this box of beautiful jewels before he died.'

All the family looked at her and the box, and they were too surprised to say a word. Virginia then took them through the secret door in the wall, and down a narrow passage, lit by a candle that Washington was carrying. At last they came to a heavy wooden door. When Virginia touched it, it opened slowly.

They found themselves in a little room with one small window in it. A skeleton lay on the floor, chained to the wall. A plate and a water jug were also on the floor, but they were too far away for the skeleton's fingers to get hold of them.

Virginia put her hands together and began to pray silently. The others looked down at the skeleton of Sir Simon de Canterville. Now they knew the terrible secret of his death.

'He is peaceful now,' said Virginia. 'I prayed to God to give him peace.'

*They took Sir Simon to the 'Garden of Death'.*

And suddenly the others were sure that they could see a beautiful light around Virginia's face.

'You are wonderful!' cried the young Duke, and he put his arm round her neck, and kissed her.

\* \* \*

Four days later, at about eleven o'clock at night, they took Sir Simon de Canterville to the 'Garden of Death', where he wanted to be. Lord Canterville came specially from Wales to be there with the Otis family.

They put Sir Simon into the ground, and Virginia put

a cross made of beautiful white flowers on the ground next to him. When she did this, the moon came out from behind a cloud, and the little night bird began to sing its sweet, high song.

Virginia was very quiet during the drive home.

The next morning, before Lord Canterville left, Mr Otis spoke to him about the box of jewels.

'My lord,' he said, 'these jewels belong to you, or to your family. Virginia asks for only one thing – the box. Can she keep it?'

'My dear sir,' replied Lord Canterville, 'your daughter has been a wonderful friend to one of my family. We shall always thank her for that. And remember, you bought the house and everything in it – the ghost, too! Anything that belonged to him is now yours. No, Mr Otis, your daughter must keep the jewels. When she is a woman, she will be happy to have pretty things to wear.'

So Virginia kept the jewels. And she wore them in the spring of 1890, when she married the young Duke of Cheshire; and everyone said, 'How beautiful!'

Some time later, she and her husband went down to Canterville Chase. One afternoon, they walked through the woods to the Garden of Death, and to the old tree.

'Virginia,' said the Duke. 'Tell me something. What happened when you were locked up with the ghost?'

'Please don't ask me, Cecil, I cannot tell you,' she said. 'Poor Sir Simon! I have much to thank him for. Yes, don't laugh, Cecil, I do. He helped me to understand about Life and Death, and that Love is stronger than both.'

The Duke kissed his wife lovingly. 'My dear, you can keep your secret. The only thing I want is your love,' he said.

'You have always had that, Cecil,' she said.

'And you will tell our children some day?'

Virginia did not answer, but her face went prettily red.

# GLOSSARY

**appear** to come where somebody can see you

**brush** *(n)* a thing that you use for cleaning the floor

**butter** a soft yellow food made from milk (often put on bread)

**candle** a stick of wax that gives light when it burns

**chain** a lot of metal rings joined together in a line

**clean** *(v)* to make something clean (not dirty)

**disappear** to go where nobody can see or find you

**Duke/Duchess** the title of an important man/woman

**faint** *(v)* to fall down suddenly, in a kind of 'sleep'

**false** not real or true

**feather** birds have feathers on their bodies to keep them warm and to help them fly

**fireplace** the place in a room where you can make a fire

**flash of lightning** a sudden bright light in the sky during a storm

**footstep** the sound of a person walking

**frighten** to make someone afraid

**garden-syringe** a machine for putting liquid onto plants

**ghost** a dead person that living people think they can see

**grass** a plant with thin green leaves that covers fields and gardens

**horrible** very bad, terrible; making you very afraid or unhappy

**housekeeper** a person whose job is to take care of another person's house

**jewel** a beautiful and expensive stone, e.g. a diamond

**jug** a container with a handle for holding water, milk, etc.

**kiss** *(v)* to touch someone with your lips in a loving way

**library** a room in a house where books are kept

**Lord** the title of a man from an important family

**medicine**   something to eat or drink that helps you to get better when you are ill

**metal**   something hard; gold, silver, steel, etc. are metals

**nutshell**   the hard outside part of a fruit that grows on a tree

**oil**   a thick liquid used to make machines work quietly and smoothly

**paint** *(n)*   a coloured liquid used to make pictures

**passage**   a narrow way in a building that goes to other rooms

**pea-shooter**   a child's toy; you blow air into it to make it shoot little balls of paper, dried peas, etc.

**peace**   a time when you have no troubles or worries

**pillow**   a soft thing to put your head on when you are in bed

**pray**   to speak to God; to ask God for something

**pretty**   nice to look at

**shape**   a thing or person that you can't see clearly

**sheet**   a big piece of thin material for a bed

**shroud**   cloth that is put around a dead body

**skeleton**   the bones of a whole person

**stain**   a dirty or coloured mark on something

**suit of armour**   a set of metal clothes that men wore in the past when they were fighting

**terror**   very great fear

**throw** (past tense **threw**)   to move your arm quickly to send something through the air

**thunder**   a very loud noise in the sky during a storm

**tremble**   to shake with cold or fear

**trick** *(n)*   a clever plan that makes somebody believe something that is not true

**turnip**   a large, hard, round white vegetable that grows under the ground

**twins**   two children born from the same mother at the same time

# The Canterville Ghost

## ACTIVITIES

## Before Reading

1  Read the back cover of the book and the story introduction on the first page. How much do you know now about the story? Tick one box for each sentence.

|  | | YES | NO |
|---|---|---|---|
| 1 | Canterville Chase is more than 300 years old. | ☐ | ☐ |
| 2 | Lord Canterville's family believes in ghosts. | ☐ | ☐ |
| 3 | The Otis family believes in ghosts. | ☐ | ☐ |
| 4 | The ghost plans to be nice to the Otis family. | ☐ | ☐ |
| 5 | The Otis twins know a lot of tricks. | ☐ | ☐ |
| 6 | Lord Canterville pays Mr Otis to take the ghost away from Canterville Chase. | ☐ | ☐ |

2  What is going to happen in the story? Can you guess? Tick one box for each sentence.

|  | | YES | NO |
|---|---|---|---|
| 1 | The Otis family try to help the ghost. | ☐ | ☐ |
| 2 | The Otis family take the ghost to America. | ☐ | ☐ |
| 3 | The ghost leaves Canterville Chase because he can't frighten anyone. | ☐ | ☐ |
| 4 | One of the Otis children helps the ghost to rest at last. | ☐ | ☐ |
| 5 | The ghost takes one of the children away from Canterville Chase. | ☐ | ☐ |

## While Reading

**Read Chapter 1. Then answer these questions.**

*What*

1 . . . did the Duchess of Bolton feel on her shoulders?
2 . . . couldn't Mr Otis buy in America?
3 . . . did the Duke of Cheshire ask Virginia?
4 . . . did Sir Simon de Canterville do in 1575?
5 . . . did Washington clean off the library floor?
6 . . . did Mrs Umney want Mr and Mrs Otis to do?

**Before you read Chapter 2, can you guess what happens? Choose answers to these questions.**

1 What will the Otis family find next morning?
  a) The ghost has killed Mrs Umney.
  b) The bloodstain is back on the library floor again.
  c) All the books in the library are on the floor.
  d) The ghost has broken the little black stick into pieces.
2 What will Mr Otis do when he meets the ghost?
  a) Tell him to leave.
  b) Sit down and talk to him.
  c) Give him a bottle of oil.
  d) Shoot him.

**Read Chapters 2 and 3. Then put these sentences into the right order, to make a short paragraph.**

1  At midnight he began to walk silently along the passage.
2  Then the ghost read the piece of paper, and understood that it was a trick.
3  He was very frightened, and ran back to his room.
4  On August 17th the ghost put on a shroud and a hat.
5  But when he touched the other ghost, its head fell off.
6  He felt very angry, but he couldn't think of a plan.
7  Early next morning he went to see the other ghost again, hoping to be its friend.
8  Suddenly he saw in front of him a horrible ghost, with eyes as red as fire.

**Read Chapter 4. Then match these halves of sentences.**

1  The ghost used oil on his chains . . .
2  One night the twins put butter on the top stair, . . .
3  When the ghost went into the twins' room, . . .
4  The ghost went down just to look at the bloodstain, . . .
5  The ghost planned to do the Horseman of Death, . . .

6  a jug of water fell down on him and he got very wet.
7  because he didn't want anyone to hear him.
8  but in the end he was too frightened to leave his room.
9  which made the ghost fall down the stairs to the bottom.
10  but the twins and Washington were waiting for him.

Read Chapter 5. Choose the best question-word for these questions, and then answer them.

*What / Where / Who / Why*

1 . . . did Virginia go up the back stairs?
2 . . . was the ghost doing when Virginia saw him?
3 . . . locked Sir Simon in a room without food or water?
4 . . . was Virginia so angry about the bloodstain?
5 . . . didn't want to go to America?
6 . . . couldn't the ghost do?
7 . . . did the ghost want to go?
8 . . . two things could Virginia do for the ghost?
9 . . . did the ghost go with Virginia?

Before you read Chapter 6, can you guess how the story ends? Choose as many of these ideas as you like.

1 Nobody ever sees Virginia again.
2 Nobody ever sees the ghost again.
3 Virginia comes back, but her hair is white.
4 The ghost is still in the house, but only Virginia can see him.
5 The ghost gives Virginia a box of beautiful jewels.
6 Virginia shows her family the skeleton of Sir Simon.
7 The Otis family go back to America with the ghost.
8 The Otis family take Sir Simon to the 'Garden of Death'.
9 Virginia marries the Duke of Cheshire.

## *After Reading*

1 **Perhaps this is what the ghost was thinking when all those terrible things happened to him. Find the right word to complete each passage, and then describe what is happening in the story at this moment.**

1 'Oh! Ouch!! Ow! I hurt everywhere. There was _____ on that top stair – I'm sure of it. Oh, those boys are going to be sorry that they did this – very, very sorry.'

2 'Where is it? It's gone – somebody's cleaned it! I'll have to make it again, but what with? Ah, what's this? I can use some of this red _____, with a bit of purple in it.'

3 'I just don't understand these people. Lord Raker's hair turned white when he heard my famous laugh, but this woman just tries to give me _____ for my stomach!'

4 'Who does this man think I am! It's my *job* to make a noise with these chains – and he tells me to put _____ on them! Oh, I haven't been so angry in years.'

5 'It's another trick! Oh, I hate them all! I had an awful night, worrying about that horrible thing, and it was just a brush under a sheet, with a _____ for a head!'

2 Find these words in the word search below, and draw lines through them. The words go from left to right, and from top to bottom.

*disappear, faint, false, feather, fireplace, frighten, ghost, horrible, jewels, jug, kiss, medicine, passage, pray, skeleton, trick*

| I | F | R | I | G | H | T | E | N | H | S | F |
|---|---|---|---|---|---|---|---|---|---|---|---|
| G | H | O | S | T | O | A | V | E | D | K | I |
| N | O | T | S | L | R | E | P | T | I | E | R |
| F | F | O | K | R | R | T | J | H | S | L | E |
| M | E | D | I | C | I | N | E | R | A | E | P |
| F | A | L | S | E | B | E | W | E | P | T | L |
| A | T | H | S | J | L | U | E | N | P | O | A |
| I | H | D | R | U | E | E | L | D | E | N | C |
| N | E | Y | E | G | P | A | S | S | A | G | E |
| T | R | I | C | K | A | R | S | P | R | A | Y |

Now write down all the letters that do not have lines through them, beginning with the first line and going across each line to the end. You will have 33 letters, which will make a sentence of 8 words.

1 What is the sentence?

2 Who said it, and to whom?

3 Who did something to change this, and what did they do?

3  Here is a new illustration for the story. Find the best place in the story to put the picture, and answer these questions.

The picture goes on page ____.

1  Which room of the house is this?
2  What is going to happen in a moment?
3  How will the ghost feel after that?

**Now write a caption for the illustration.**

*Caption:* _____

**4 Put these sentences in the right order to tell the story of Sir Simon de Canterville.**

1 When the Otis family arrived, the ghost had a difficult time.

2 His wife's brothers locked him in a room without food or water, and he died there.

3 Then Virginia met the ghost, and prayed for him to die.

4 For 300 years he was the best ghost in the country.

5 Sir Simon murdered his wife in the library in 1575.

6 After that, Sir Simon's ghost never appeared again.

7 After that, his ghost began to appear in Canterville Chase.

8 The family found Sir Simon's skeleton, and put it in the ground in the 'Garden of Death'.

9 Then, in 1584, he suddenly disappeared.

**5 These are some of the ways that Sir Simon liked to appear. Which is the most frightening and which is the least frightening, do you think? Put them in order.**

- as a big black dog
- as a skeleton
- wearing heavy chains
- with no head
- in a shroud, smelling of death

**What is the most frightening kind of ghost that you can think of? Complete this sentence.**

I think the most frightening ghost is one that _____.

# ABOUT THE AUTHOR

Oscar Wilde was born in Dublin in 1854. He went to college there and then studied at Oxford, where in 1878 he won a poetry prize. In 1883 he went to the USA and stayed there for a year, travelling around the country and giving talks. In 1884 he got married, and in 1888 he wrote *The Happy Prince and Other Tales*, a book of stories for his sons. *The Canterville Ghost* was one of the stories in a book called *Lord Arthur Savile's Crime and Other Stories*, published in 1891.

Wilde wrote one novel, *The Picture of Dorian Gray* (1890), but he is best known for his plays. His first two plays did not do well, but the third, *Lady Windermere's Fan* (1892), was funny and clever, and people loved it. His greatest play, *The Importance of Being Earnest*, appeared in 1895, but in that same year he was sent to prison because of his relationship with another man, Lord Alfred Douglas. When he came out in 1897, he went to live in France, where he wrote *The Ballad of Reading Gaol* (1898), a long poem about his time in prison. He died in Paris in 1900.

Wilde's plays, fairy-tales, and stories are still very popular today. He was a wonderful storyteller, whether writing or speaking, and in his day he was famous for his clever and amusing conversation. One friend, the poet W. B. Yeats, called him 'the greatest talker of his time', and another friend described how Oscar Wilde took away his bad toothache one day – just by telling him stories and making him laugh.

# OXFORD BOOKWORMS LIBRARY

*Classics • Crime & Mystery • Factfiles • Fantasy & Horror*
*Human Interest • Playscripts • Thriller & Adventure*
*True Stories • World Stories*

The OXFORD BOOKWORMS LIBRARY provides enjoyable reading in English, with a wide range of classic and modern fiction, non-fiction, and plays. It includes original and adapted texts in seven carefully graded language stages, which take learners from beginner to advanced level. An overview is given on the next pages.

All Stage 1 titles are available as audio recordings, as well as over eighty other titles from Starter to Stage 6. All Starters and many titles at Stages 1 to 4 are specially recommended for younger learners. Every Bookworm is illustrated, and Starters and Factfiles have full-colour illustrations.

The OXFORD BOOKWORMS LIBRARY also offers extensive support. Each book contains an introduction to the story, notes about the author, a glossary, and activities. Additional resources include tests and worksheets, and answers for these and for the activities in the books. There is advice on running a class library, using audio recordings, and the many ways of using Oxford Bookworms in reading programmes. Resource materials are available on the website <www.oup.com/bookworms>.

The *Oxford Bookworms Collection* is a series for advanced learners. It consists of volumes of short stories by well-known authors, both classic and modern. Texts are not abridged or adapted in any way, but carefully selected to be accessible to the advanced student.

---

You can find details and a full list of titles in the *Oxford Bookworms Library Catalogue* and *Oxford English Language Teaching Catalogues*, and on the website <www.oup.com/bookworms>.

# THE OXFORD BOOKWORMS LIBRARY
## GRADING AND SAMPLE EXTRACTS

### STARTER • 250 HEADWORDS

present simple – present continuous – imperative –
*can/cannot, must* – *going to* (future) – simple gerunds ...

Her phone is ringing – but where is it?

Sally gets out of bed and looks in her bag. No phone. She looks under the bed. No phone. Then she looks behind the door. There is her phone. Sally picks up her phone and answers it. *Sally's Phone*

### STAGE 1 • 400 HEADWORDS

... past simple – coordination with *and*, *but*, *or* –
subordination with *before*, *after*, *when*, *because*, *so* ...

I knew him in Persia. He was a famous builder and I worked with him there. For a time I was his friend, but not for long. When he came to Paris, I came after him – I wanted to watch him. He was a very clever, very dangerous man. *The Phantom of the Opera*

### STAGE 2 • 700 HEADWORDS

... present perfect – *will* (future) – *(don't) have to, must not, could* –
comparison of adjectives – simple *if* clauses – past continuous –
tag questions – *ask/tell* + infinitive ...

While I was writing these words in my diary, I decided what to do. I must try to escape. I shall try to get down the wall outside. The window is high above the ground, but I have to try. I shall take some of the gold with me – if I escape, perhaps it will be helpful later. *Dracula*

*… should, may* – present perfect continuous – *used to* – past perfect –
causative – relative clauses – indirect statements …

Of course, it was most important that no one should see
Colin, Mary, or Dickon entering the secret garden. So Colin
gave orders to the gardeners that they must all keep away
from that part of the garden in future. ***The Secret Garden***

### STAGE 4 • 1400 HEADWORDS

*… past perfect continuous – passive (simple forms) –
would* conditional clauses – indirect questions –
relatives with *where/when* – gerunds after prepositions/phrases …

I was glad. Now Hyde could not show his face to the world
again. If he did, every honest man in London would be proud
to report him to the police. ***Dr Jekyll and Mr Hyde***

### STAGE 5 • 1800 HEADWORDS

*… future continuous – future perfect –
passive (modals, continuous forms) –
would have* conditional clauses – modals + perfect infinitive …

If he had spoken Estella's name, I would have hit him. I was so
angry with him, and so depressed about my future, that I could
not eat the breakfast. Instead I went straight to the old house.
***Great Expectations***

### STAGE 6 • 2500 HEADWORDS

*…* passive (infinitives, gerunds) – advanced modal meanings –
clauses of concession, condition

When I stepped up to the piano, I was confident. It was as if I
knew that the prodigy side of me really did exist. And when I
started to play, I was so caught up in how lovely I looked that
I didn't worry how I would sound. ***The Joy Luck Club***

# Alice's Adventures in Wonderland

## LEWIS CARROLL

*Retold by Jennifer Bassett*

There, on top of the mushroom, was a large caterpillar, smoking a pipe. After a while the Caterpillar took the pipe out of its mouth and said to Alice in a slow, sleepy voice, 'Who are you?'

What strange things happen when Alice falls down the rabbit-hole and into Wonderland! She has conversations with the Caterpillar and the Cheshire Cat, goes to the Mad Hatter's tea party, plays croquet with the King and Queen of Hearts ...

# The Children of the New Forest

## CAPTAIN MARRYAT

*Retold by Rowena Akinyemi*

England in 1647: King Charles is in prison, and Cromwell's men are fighting the King's men. These are dangerous times for everybody.

The four Beverley children have no parents; their mother is dead and their father died while fighting for the King. Now Cromwell's soldiers have come to burn the house – with the children in it.

The four of them escape into the New Forest – but how will they live? What will they eat? And will Cromwell's soldiers find them?